MW00411694

Ready or Not,
Here Comes School!

Preparing Your Child
From Newborn to School Age

Dr. Barbara Sorrels

Dedication

I dedicate this book to all of the teachers who diligently and faithfully seek to educate ALL of the children entrusted to their care—the gifted and talented; the abused and neglected; homeless and frightened; the rich and the poor; the special needs children with autism, dyslexia, ADD and ADHD.

You seek to find the best in each child and call forth their God given talents and abilities.

I also dedicate it to the parents who nurture their children well, in a culture that leads them to believe they need to leave the education of their children to the "experts."

You carry out your calling to parent well with grace and courage, providing teaching and instruction to help your children find their God-given purpose.

About Dr. Barbara

Dr. Barbara Sorrels' own experience as a parent, teacher, caregiver, university professor, consultant, and children's pastor brings a unique and relatable quality to her work, speaking, and writing.

"I help parents and teachers understand what makes kids tick by "looking under the hood" and understanding basic principles of child development. I've seen that scientific research actually bears out truths of scripture."

Parents are bombarded by a variety of conflicting messages that often leave them confused. Understanding God's amazing design and a child's need for nurturing relationships helps parents see each child's uniqueness – and how to love and nurture them well. The result is deeper connections among family members, less conflict, and happier children and parents.

Dr. Barbara is Executive Director of The Institute for Childhood Education, a private professional development and consulting firm for those who live and work with children. Dr. Sorrels has had over twenty years of classroom experience teaching children of all ages in child care, kindergarten, and elementary school classrooms, as well as over five years' experience teaching graduate and undergraduate students at the University level.

She also founded and directed early childhood centers located in Washington, D. C. and Fort Worth, Texas.

Dr. Sorrels holds a doctorate in Early Childhood Education from Oklahoma State University, a master's degree in Christian Education from Southwestern Seminary, and a bachelor's degree from the University of Maryland. She served for over five years on the faculty of Oklahoma State University teaching in the Early Child Education program.

She is married to Bob Sorrels, and they have two daughters and one granddaughter.

www.DrBarbaraSorrels.com

**Contact us to discuss having Dr. Barbara speak
at your conference, church, or event:**

www.DrBarbaraSorrels.com

Contents

1. School Readiness: More than ABC's and 1, 2, 3's .. 1

2. School Readiness Begins Before Birth 5

3. The Power of Relationships 7

4. The Gift of Language 11

5. Phonemic Awareness 17

6. A Sense of Autonomy 19

7. Self-Regulation 25

8. Curiosity 35

9. Laying a Foundation for Math 39

10. Literacy 43

11. Social Skills 47

12. The Right Start 51

    Summary 55

Chapter 1

School Readiness: More than ABC's and 1, 2, 3's

Is my child ready for school? Every August millions of parents across America silently ask themselves this question as they send their children off to school for the first time. Will my son be left behind or will my daughter be sidelined in the race to the top? Anxious parents buy computer games, flashcards, CD's and Baby Einstein videos that claim to make their child smarter and prepare them for school. In some parts of the country, preschool enrollment has turned into a high stakes competition. Parents camp out on the street for a chance to enroll their three-year-old in a "prestigious" preschool that charges the equivalent of college tuition, with the belief that it will give their child a leg up in life and increase their chances of getting into an Ivy League school. Is this much ado about nothing or is there truth to this belief?

Before we look at the topic of school readiness I must first tell you that the question, "Is my child ready for school?" should never be asked without also asking the question, "Is the school ready for my child?" In our culture we put the burden of "readiness" on the child when, in fact, the burden should rest on families and schools. Schools have a moral and ethical obligation to prepare themselves to meet the needs of the families and children that they serve. Some schools seriously consider their own readiness and do a phenomenal job of "crossing the street" so to speak to meet the needs of individual families and children. But all too often both public and private schools smugly uphold their "standards" and beckon children and families to jump through their hoops without doing the hard work of self-reflection and evaluation of their own preparedness. However, the readiness of schools is a topic for another day. Let's focus on how families can help to prepare children for school.

The First Day of School

As a teacher, I loved the first day of school with the hope and optimism of a new beginning and the chance to do it better one more time. I stood at the door, greeting my children, watching their faces as we came together to embark on a new year together. For most, eagerness and anticipation was the order of the day; but for a few, their eyes betrayed a hint of apprehension and fear. My goal on the first day was to create a relaxed and welcoming atmosphere and to provide activities that would help me become acquainted with the children. I wanted to know what was important to them; what sparked their interest and curiosity, and to begin to assess what they already knew and where I needed to take them next. It always surprised me how small and vulnerable they looked on the first day...not the confident, "big" kids I sent home on the last day of school in June.

One of the children in particular caught my attention. My radar cranked up a notch. She was quite smaller than the rest, highly social and bubbly. Julie was the definition of "perpetual motion." She chattered constantly, wiggled and giggled and skipped about the room as if she had not a care in the world. I secretly loved her "every day is a party" demeanor but it wasn't always compatible with my primary task of trying to teach her something. During group times she wanted to wander the classroom and do her own thing.

2

She disrupted other children with her constant talking. She loved silly talk and made up silly rhymes. She walked on her tiptoes and was very braggadocios—small signs that made me begin to suspect that she was really much younger than six. By the end of the first six weeks my radar was on high alert and I suspected that something was amiss.

To make a long story short, we eventually discovered that mom had forged a birth certificate and lied about Julie's age in order to enroll her in first grade. Julie was actually four-years-old and when mom was confronted she defended her deception by claiming she had a genius on her hands because she knew her alphabet and could count to 100. She insisted that her daughter was "ready" for school. This mom didn't understand that reciting the ABC's and 1, 2, 3's has very little to do with reading and mathematical understanding. It just means they have a good memory.

So, what does it mean for a child to be "ready" for school? Popular advertising would have you believe that knowing letters, numbers, colors, sounds and shapes is the essence of school readiness. Look at the racks of every discount and bookstore in America and you will find workbooks proclaiming to teach "readiness skills." Look at the walls of typical preschool and kindergarten classrooms. They are adorned with the ABC's and 1, 2, 3's, and charts with colors and shapes, so it is only natural that parents would assume this is the magic key and "knowledge worth knowing." The truth is that a child could know these things and still not be "ready" for school. **School readiness means that a child has the capacity to successfully function within a group environment that is primarily focused on education.** Readiness for school is far more dependent upon emotional and social factors than on academic skills.

Chapter 2

School Readiness Begins Before Birth

Research over the last several decades has revealed that the developing brain is far more fragile than ever expected. It was assumed that the baby was safely tucked away in a cocoon-like environment protected from harm. Scientists now know that the baby is extremely vulnerable to environmental and experiential factors both inside and outside of the womb. School readiness begins in utero. The two primary ingredients required to grow a healthy baby are oxygen and healthy nutrition. A healthy diet is crucial for a pregnant mom and a smoke free existence is key. Smoking robs the baby of oxygen, which is critical in the development of a healthy brain.

Another thing that we have learned is that chronic and severe stress during pregnancy threatens healthy development. Stress hormones cross the placenta and can do harm. Stressed out moms have stressed out babies.

Lastly, freedom from toxic substances is critical. One of the most destructive and prevalent toxins is alcohol. Despite claims made on popular websites for pregnant moms, **there is no amount of alcohol that can be safely ingested during pregnancy.** Prenatal alcohol exposure causes varying degrees of irreparable brain damage and sets children up for learning problems. Memory loss, difficulty with information processing, and an inability to understand cause and effect relationships are just some of the manifestations of alcohol exposure. The effects of alcohol range from mild to severe. The timing and the amount of alcohol intake are the deciding factors in the amount of damage done. A little bit of alcohol at a critical point in development—primarily the first trimester before many women even know they are pregnant—can profoundly alter the development of a healthy brain. Learning difficulties due to alcohol exposure are 100% preventable. Mothers simply should not drink alcohol during pregnancy.

A young mom recently came to me for help with her 4-year-old adopted daughter. The child had documented severe, prenatal exposure to alcohol and was struggling in her Pre-K program both academically and behaviorally. Her sweet mom described a common dynamic that played out in their home on a regular basis: "I put her in time out for doing something. When she gets up I tell her what she did wrong and not to do it again. Then she gets up and does exactly what I told her not to do as if she doesn't understand what I'm saying."

She looked at me in shock when I told her, "She doesn't understand. She hears the words but she doesn't have the capacity to link hitting someone to sitting in time out." Making connections is the essence of intelligence and prenatal alcohol seriously disrupts a child's ability to make connections between ideas and events. Alcohol has the potential of severely altering the trajectory of a culture in one generation.

Chapter 3

The Power of Relationships

Joey struggled to learn to read in first grade. I tried every approach I could think of and nothing seemed to click. I invited the parents to have a conference with me to brainstorm and work together to help this little boy succeed, but they refused. The dad wrote me a letter that said it was an ego trip for teachers to tell parents about their kids and they would not be attending a conference now or ever. I made games for Joey to hopefully play at home with his parents but the envelopes came back unopened. Joey would often look at me with sad eyes and say, "My mommy and daddy don't care if I learn to read." He often fell asleep in class and was sent to school ill. I tried everything I could possibly think of to spark this child's interest in reading. Finally, after Christmas I hit on an idea and Joey slowly began to make progress. This child's struggle was not due to a lack of intelligence; his struggle was due to a lack of secure, warm, responsive relationships at home and his belief that no one cared.

A loving and attentive parent is the most important "readiness" tool that a child can have. In other words, it boils down to relationships. Sounds simple enough but unfortunately in the culture in which we live having a relationship with your child is often more difficult than it seems. I believe that the majority of America's children are at risk of emotional starvation due to poverty of relationships.

7

The greatest threat to a child's wellbeing today is preoccupied parents. Some are preoccupied for understandable reasons—illness, catastrophic injury and poverty sap adult attention and energy. For others, materialism that masquerades as "success" takes precedence over the children. Kids intrinsically know where they are on the priority list. They instinctively know when mom and dad are working long hours every day to put food on the table, versus working to buy that boat or membership in the exclusive country club. It's not that these things are bad for children in and of themselves, but when acquiring things takes precedence over our children, it becomes toxic to healthy relationships.

In every interaction we have with our children, we send them a message that communicates our feelings toward them. They hear in our tone of voice, see in our body language and feel in our touch something of their value in our eyes. When we don't get off the cell phone long enough to greet our children while picking them up from child care, we send them a message. When we grab them by the arm and push them down hard in the grocery cart, we send them a message. When we roll our eyes at their questions and grit our teeth as we give a terse response, we send them a message.

Uri Bronnfenbrenner once said that, "every child needs to know there is someone who is truly crazy about him." A child's belief that he is worthy of love and care is the basis of mental health and learning. But how does this influence learning? The emotional closeness and psychological intimacy found in a healthy parent-child relationship provides a secure base from which the child is able to venture out into the world with confidence and optimism. Their belief that the world is a safe place where others can be trusted to meet their needs allows them to invest their emotional energy in exploration and learning rather than merely coping. Children who can rest secure in the knowledge that they are the apple of someone's eye can whole heartedly embrace the world and

8

all that the learning environment has to offer. They have the courage to try new things and take risks because they have the confidence that someone has their back.

A warm and loving home environment provides a place of retreat when the world becomes stressful and overwhelming. Even navigating the school day in the best of schools can be exhausting for a young child. There are typically multiple transitions and many expectations from many different people. Home should a place where the child finds psychological safety and a place to regain his moorings. Children with responsive and loving parents recover from stressful situations more quickly than the child who lives in relational chaos. Without warm loving relationships development and learning are compromised.

Chapter 4

The Gift of Language

I love listening to the chatter of children at play. They talk, sing and chant their way through the day. Language development is a predictor of school success. Children who know lots of words and know how to use those words to make requests, tell stories, give explanations, ask questions and enjoy conversation are more likely to be successful in school than children who know few words and little about how to use them. Research has revealed that the first three years of life is a "sensitive period" or prime time for learning language.

Babies are born with the capacity to learn multiple languages. They have the potential to learn any language known to man. When parents chant, sing, read and talk to an infant his brain forms connections for learning that particular language. The number, strength, and complexity of those connections is directly proportionate to the amount of language he hears. It is like a computer in terms of data in, data out. A child who is spoken to a lot will have lots of connections. A child who is spoken to a little will have few connections.

The brain is a very efficient organ and wants to run as quickly and proficiently as possible. So by the end of the third year, the brain begins to prune or eliminate the connections that are not needed. If a child lives in an environment where he only hears English, there is no need to maintain the connections for speaking French or German so they begin to fade. It does not mean that a child cannot learn a language after the age of three—it simply means that the younger the child is, the easier it is to learn language. By age three the trajectory of a child's language development is pretty much set. Children with big vocabularies will typically continue to acquire more language. Those who have a small vocabulary and limited command of the English language will typically continue to fall behind and struggle in school unless there is a very intensive and costly intervention.

How does a small vocabulary and limited language impact success in school? When a child gets on the bus in the morning, most likely he is not thinking about all of the wonderful things he is going to learn that day. Typically he is wondering who he is going to play with at recess or sit by at lunch. Children are usually more concerned about the social aspects of school, rather than the academics. Relationships with other children are highly dependent upon language. Those who struggle with language are often excluded from play because they aren't able to contribute ideas, negotiate roles and navigate the relational challenges that are inevitable with this age. School is a lonely and drab place to be when you have no friends and a child's emotional energies are spent on merely coping rather than learning. Children with limited language also struggle with being able to understand what they read or what is read to them. They are unable to tell and retell stories, grasp concepts and enjoy typical classroom discussions.

So how can parents create a language rich environment and build those language connections? Though the first three years are critical, it is important to create a rich language environment throughout childhood.

- Read to your child every day, including your infant. Around 6 weeks of age a baby's field of vision expands to be able to at least briefly look at a single object book. As your child grows, find books that your child loves to have read over and over again. Most communities have free libraries. Take advantage of this valuable resource. Many libraries allow young children to get a library card. Find out the requirements for your particular library and get yourself and your child a card.

• Sing to your baby and to your children. Take a familiar tune and make up your own words. Listen to kid songs in the car and sing along.

• Be a "sports caster" for your infant. You can't have a reciprocal conversation with a baby but you can talk to her in a meaningful way by narrating what she does much like a sports caster narrates a football game. "Look at Nora roll the ball. Go get it…look at Nora run to get the ball. She's got it! Yeah!!! Now she rolls it to daddy."

• Talk about things that are important to your child. Look him in the eye and give him your full presence. Allow him to take the lead and talk about what is on his mind.

• See my web site for a video example called "Eating Snakes":
http://www.drbarbarasorrels.com/here-comes-school/

• Introduce big words. When my daughter was two we taught her that food is not just good, it is "delectable." We were eating dinner with some friends one night when she piped up and said to our hostess, "The food is delectable." Our friends were shocked that a two year old would know this word. Take an ordinary word and brainstorm as many words that have a similar meaning. For example, synonyms for the word happy can be joyful, delighted, pleased, contented, glad or cheery.

• Give children lots to talk about. Children who live in sterile surroundings with limited life experiences have little to talk about. A child who is parked in front of a television, computer or electronic game will have little reason for conversation. Sadly, many children interact with machines more than they interact with people. Likewise, a single-minded focus on academic skills gives children little to talk about. When they are endlessly drilled on letters, numbers, colors, sounds and shapes, they have little opportunity to develop a rich vocabulary. The more real life experiences a child has, the more they have to talk about.

- Families who are able to take vacations to the mountains, lakes, desserts or oceans expose children to different environments and that introduces different words and concepts about the world. But providing a rich variety of experiences need not be costly and only for the wealthy. People with meager means can have "ready" children by taking advantage of the free and ordinary experiences of daily life in the community. It means that everywhere you go, you look for the learning. Take your toddler to the park and eat lunch on a blanket. Feel and talk about the texture of the grass. Listen for the sounds of nature. Collect rocks, look for insects and watch for birds; observe the ants that are trying to carry away your chips. Visit a shoe store and talk about the shoes you would wear to a party, the shoes you would wear on a walk in woods, or the shoes you would wear in the rain. Talk about the colors, the textures and the material that the shoes are made of. Compare the different kinds of soles and why sports shoes have thicker soles than dress shoes. You get the picture. It's about the grown-ups changing their perspective on ordinary life.

- Visit the zoo, public library or museum. Pick wildflowers in a field. Collect fireflies at night. Visit public

14

playgrounds. Feed the ducks at a local park. Visit the grocery store and observe and talk about the different kinds of fruits and vegetables. Everywhere you go introduce new words, new concepts and new ways of looking at the world.

- Eat dinner together at least 4 times a week and tell stories about your day. The family dinner is nearly obsolete in America. Research abounds on the many contributions the family meal makes to the healthy development of children but one of the prime advantages is language development. Children learn the art of conversation and how to listen, take turns and exchange ideas. Sounds simple enough but many children have no idea how to do this because they have never had the opportunity.

Chapter 5

Phonemic Awareness

By the age of four, most children are very proud of their newfound ability to use the English language and they chatter non-stop. They chant, they sing, they make up silly jokes and rhymes and ask millions of questions. Most four-year olds love Dr. Seuss who is known as the "king of rhyme." Though the educational content of a Dr. Seuss books is sometimes debated there is no doubt that he got it right when it comes to the appeal of rhyme.

Phonemic awareness, defined as the ability to manipulate discrete sounds in the English language, predicts success in reading. In plain English, this means that the ability to identify rhyming words at age four indicates the child is likely to be a successful reader. Please note that the age at which the typical child can hear and identify rhyme is four—not three, not two or younger. This does not mean that we don't introduce rhyming words to younger children or that there won't be children who master this skill much earlier. But it is not considered the "norm" until age four.

- Beginning in infancy, introduce infants and children to nursery rhymes, rhyming stories, songs and chants.

- Play silly games with your child. For example, insert a nonsensical rhyming word into a sentence and see if your child notices. "Get into the star so we can drive to the store."

- Think of real words and nonsense words that rhyme with your child's name.

- Play word games with rhyme. For example, "I'm thinking of a word that rhymes with tree. It striped. It flies. It buzzes. (A bee)

- Read Dr. Seuss books and enjoy the silliness.

Chapter 6

A Sense of Autonomy

It was the first day of school and I was talking to the children about the many things they would be doing in first grade. One of them asked if they were going to learn to read, which sparked a great deal of discussion and excitement. As the children worked at their desks, drawing pictures of something they wanted to share about their summer, Ryan approached me with a quivering chin and a look of fear in his eyes. "I don't know how to read," he blurted out as big tears rolled down his checks. I put my arm around him and reassured him that most of the children didn't know how to read and it was okay. I promised that I would help him every step of the way and when the time was right, he would be reading. He calmed down and went back to his drawing.

From across the room a child asked me how to spell the word, "fish." He wanted to label his drawing of the fish that he caught that summer. Upon hearing this, Ryan shot out of his chair and approached me again with the same fearful look. "I don't know how to spell either," he said choking back tears. Once again, I reassured him that he wasn't supposed to know how to spell yet. As the year went on, little Ryan struggled, not because he lacked intelligence but because he lacked a sense of autonomy. He had little confidence in his ability to do things for himself and to learn. As I got to know Ryan's mom, I understood some of the reasons why he was fearful and clingy. He was a sickly baby with many allergies and his parents divorced shortly after he was born. He was all mom had. Her constant worry about his health drove her to try to protect him from all manner of disappointment, stress and struggle. In her well-meaning attempts to be a good mom, her anxiety spilled over onto Ryan which set him up for insecurity and self-doubt.

Children are born with an innate drive to explore and master the world. Just watch a time lapse of this nine-month-old baby as he explores the dining room of his home.

See my web site for a video example called "Time Lapse":

http://www.drbarbarasorrels.com/here-comes-school/

As you can see, this little guy explores every square inch of the room, from the cobwebs in the corner to the empty cardboard box. Children who are encouraged to explore and master the world develop a sense of "autonomy." They approach life with a sense of confidence and competence, knowing that they are able to do things for themselves. Autonomy does not mean that a child is allowed to rule the roost and do what he pleases. It means that the child is encouraged to try new things, take risks and explore. **Autonomous children approach learning with confidence--an, "I can do it!" attitude that motives them to embrace school with gusto.** They aren't afraid to ask for help when they need it, but they are able to navigate the school day with relative independence.

How do parents encourage autonomy? It begins in infancy by creating a child-friendly home that encourages exploration and discovery. Baby gates should only be used to protect the child from danger, not to maintain the pristine appearance of the home. The goal is to create an environment where you can say, "yes" most of the time. Enriched environments don't have to be expensive and parents don't have to run out and buy all kind of gadgets and gizmos with flashing lights and sound. The normal, everyday objects found around a typical household provide a wealth of things to explore. Remove anything that would be harmful as well as things of personal value that you want to protect. Otherwise, allow your child to safely explore the ordinary contents of the home. For example, rearrange your kitchen so that the lower cabinets contain plastic ware or other kitchen items that are safe for your little ones. When my daughter was an infant her favorite "hat" was the Tupperware lettuce keeper that she dragged out from the cabinets. Playpens and other baby contraptions that confine infants should only be used for short periods of time when the safety of the child is the primary concern—not the convenience of the parent.

A second factor in fostering autonomy is allowing children to face "manageable challenges." There is a phenomenon today called, "helicopter parenting." I first heard this term when I took my first daughter to college. These are parents who hover over their children in order to protect them from any degree of frustration, disappointment or pain. Though they are well meaning, helicopter parents undermine their child's development.

Self-esteem doesn't happen when we pat kids on the back and tell them how awesome they are or give every child on the team a trophy because we don't want to psychologically damage them. It also doesn't mean that we never say "no" and give in to all of their demands for fear of scarring them for life. Children develop self-esteem by meeting manageable challenges. It means letting a child struggle with a puzzle or building materials until they finally accomplish their goal. It means allowing and insisting children do for themselves what they are capable of doing and not stepping in to do it for them because it is faster or more convenient.

But what is the difference between a manageable

challenge and one that is overwhelming and potentially damaging?

I recently had this conversation with a mom who had adopted a child from an orphanage. Her five-year old daughter had experienced extreme deprivation in the first two years of life, which had profound implications for the behavior and daily life of this beautiful little girl.

She was enrolled in a camp that I was leading for children who had come from hard places. The child had difficulty separating from mom the first day of camp and Mom's anxiety was apparent.

I pulled her aside to reassure her that her daughter was going to be okay. She expressed her fear of re-traumatizing this child who had already seen more trauma in her short life than many will ever see in a life time.

We talked about the difference between a manageable challenge and a traumatic experience. A manageable challenge is one in which the child has the inner or external resources to cope. A traumatic experience is one in which the child does not have the internal or external resources to cope and the situation is emotionally overwhelming.

For example, a child is putting a puzzle together for the first time and is beginning to show some frustration. He sighs, slumps his shoulders and looks anxiously about. I read the body language and pause to observe for further signs of stress.

But suddenly his face lights up, he picks up a puzzle piece and successfully adds it to the puzzle and goes on to complete it by himself. He has successfully met the challenge through his own inner resources.

Or, let's assume he continues to exhibit stress behaviors. He sighs again, puffs out his lip, picks up a piece and throws it down and glares at the puzzle. His stress is obviously escalating.

I sit down next to him and offer a clue that might help.

"Look at the color of the policeman's raincoat. Do you see any more yellow pieces?" He scans the table and quickly finds another yellow piece that fits.

His demeanor returns to a state of calm and he is back on track to finish the puzzle. This child has just met a manageable challenge with a minimal amount of external support. These are the kinds of experiences that help children grow. I would have robbed the child of a chance to grow had I stepped in and completed the puzzle for him.

Children who have been given the opportunity to face manageable challenges are able to persevere when learning new things. They don't get discouraged and give up easily; they keep on keeping on until they get it. It stands to reason then, that autonomous children find more enjoyment and pleasure in school and demonstrate a higher level of creativity and flexibility in thinking.

On the other hand, many children face challenges every day for which they do not have the capacity to manage.

Teachers aren't supposed to have favorites but one year there was a little third grader that made it really hard for me not to break this cardinal rule.

Casey was born to very young parents who divorced when he was two. One morning he arrived at school extremely agitated and volatile. Before the bell even rang to start the day he had picked a couple of fights and it became obvious that he was unable to focus on his work.

I took him aside and said, "Casey, you are having a really bad morning. Did something happen at home?" He burst into tears and blurted out, "My mom said she isn't going to cook dinner for me anymore and she's not going to wash my clothes." Verging on hysteria he said, "I don't know how to cook and I can't reach the dial on the washer."

He was traumatized because he knew he didn't have the necessary resources. This was an unmanageable challenge and the sort of thing that undermines healthy emotional development and learning.

So how can a parent support a child's autonomy?

- Child proof your home and design it so children have the freedom to explore most of it without fear of harm or breaking things. Put child safe items in lower cabinets and drawers.

- Move closet rods down to the child's level so he can hang up his own clothes.

- Provide low shelves and drawers so children can easily put things away.

- Teach your preschooler self-help skills: how to zip, button, fasten his coat and clothing, tie his shoes, put on hats, gloves and mittens.

- Teach your child how to put on a coat by himself.

- See my web site for a video example called "Putting on a coat":
  http://www.drbarbarasorrels.com/here-comes-school/

- Give children age-appropriate choices. For example, it would not be appropriate to ask a young child if he wants to go to bed but it would be appropriate to ask him if he wants to wear red jammies or blue jammies.

Chapter 7

Self-Regulation

My daughter's first year of teaching was in an at-risk school. As is the case in most American cities, we put our least experienced teachers in the most challenging settings. Though she graduated at the top of her class and by all standards was a deeply committed and knowledgeable teacher, she struggled to help the children find success in school. We had regular phone conversations debriefing her day.

She struggled to understand why her children could typically perform well when she was working with them one-on-one but acted as if they knew nothing when they were sitting in class. Were these children lacking in intelligence? Obviously not, because they could do the work when they were given her undivided attention. These children were lacking in self-regulation skills, not intelligence. When I sat in the back of the classroom to observe, they made faces at each other, drummed their pencils, pinched, poked and prodded each other. They would fly off the handle when someone looked at them "funny," and they noticed every movement, whisper and shuffle of every child in the room.

They were unable to screen out unimportant stimuli and pay attention to the one thing that was important. They were lacking in what we call "self-regulation." Self-regulation is key to successful functioning in both school and in life.

The foundation of this important capacity is established in the first three years. There are many aspects and nuances of what we call self-regulation but we will take a look at just three: focused attention, working memory and impulse control.

The ability to pay attention has been found to be the strongest predictor of school success. How do we teach children to focus for long periods of time? The answer may be surprising to some—children develop long attention spans through play. When children play, they engage in activities and tasks that are enjoyable to them. They often lose themselves in what they are doing and become oblivious to anything else around them. They don't play for very long with something that they don't like.

I have often heard people say that children can attend for only one minute per year of age. A two year old can only attend for two minutes, a three year old for only three minutes and so on. I say hogwash. They only have short attention spans when they aren't interested in what is before them.

When my daughter was eighteen-months-old she took her sister's thirty-two piece cardboard puzzle behind an overstuffed chair in the corner of our living room one morning and proceeded to dump it out. Expecting her to either get extremely frustrated or quickly move on to something else I surreptitiously peaked behind the chair to observe what she was doing. She spent much of the morning slowly putting the pieces in place. She'd try one, discover it wouldn't work, put it down and find another. By lunchtime she had it back together, coming out from behind the chair only to get a diaper change, a snack or a drink.

Much to my amazement, she spent all of her waking hours that day taking apart and putting the puzzle together over and over again. By about 7 PM, she could put it together in just a couple of minutes. Is she a genius? No. She is a typical developing child at the intersection of interest

26

and opportunity—two ingredients necessary for focused attention.

When children are given the opportunity to be involved with materials and activities that captivate their interests they will maintain focused attention for long periods of time even at very young ages. Does this mean that we need to buy expensive toys for our kids? No, not at all. I once met a Native American man who told me he was given the gift of poverty. He grew up in a stick house with a dirt floor. They had few store-bought materials but this, he said, motivated him to be resourceful. He invented games with sticks and rocks. They used hollow logs and stumps to make music. They used their imagination to be pirates and princesses. This man grew up to be a doctor and he attributes his success to his early years of material poverty.

Does this mean that we don't buy children toys? No, but it means we carefully choose the toys we buy. As a general rule, toys with flashing lights, colors and sounds don't hold children's attention for very long. Things that allow children to use their imagination and use the materials in creative and flexible ways keep children engaged. We call these "open-ended" because there is no right or wrong way to use them. Blocks, art materials and Legos are examples of open-ended toys. Adding "loose parts" to store-bought materials will extend the play and capture children's interest and attention. Adding pieces of fabric, Pringle cans, toilet paper tubes or hair rollers to the blocks brings a new dimension to the play.

Another important ingredient is time. We live in a fast paced society and time is a precious commodity in most homes. **Children are not meant to be hurried.** Many behavioral problems with young children can be attributed to hurrying them. Complex and focused play emerges over time and will not happen instantaneously. Carving out time for play is critical.

In the name of "school readiness" many preschool programs have adopted an academic approach to supposedly get children "ready for school." Worksheets, teacher directed activities with a focus on letters, numbers, colors, sounds, and shapes have become common. Don't be duped by their claims. A heavy focus on academics in the early years is more likely to undermine focused attention than support it. Worksheets and academic skills rarely hold a child's attention for longer than several minutes. Carefully observe your child, follow his lead and he will show you through his behavior what is of interest to him.

Working memory is the second aspect of self-regulation. Working memory is the ability to remember information long enough to use it in some way. When we call information to get a phone number and hold it in our mind long enough to dial it, we are using our working memory. Working memory is essential for successful functioning in a school environment. Throughout the day children are called upon to follow multiple step directions. "Johnny, put on your coat and line up to go outside to play." Johnny may put on his coat but by the time he accomplishes this task he has forgotten what he is supposed to do next so he ends up wandering around the classroom. Sometimes children like Johnny are labeled "defiant" or "uncooperative" when that isn't the case at all.

A lack of working memory can impact learning as well as behavior. When children are learning to "decode" or sound out words, those with a weak working memory will forget the beginning sounds of a word by the time they get to the end. It's as if information slips through their mind like a sieve.

There are many playful ways that parents can help strengthen this important skill:

• Play "I'm going on a trip…" while riding in the car. Start with the first letter of the alphabet. "I'm going on a trip and I'm going to take an apple." The next person has to think of something with letter B but must first identify the item that starts with A. "I'm going on a trip and I am going to take an apple and a bathing suit." The next person would say, "I'm going on a trip and I am going to take an apple, a bathing suit and a coat." Make up similar games to play as a family.

- Play 20 questions. Someone thinks of an object and the others ask questions to try to guess what that object is. Children have to remember the clues to make a logical guess.

- Play commercially purchased or home-made memory games.

- Play "What's Missing?" Gather a random assortment of objects from around the house and put them on a tray. Have children close their eyes and remove one of the objects. They have to guess which object was removed from the tray.

- Clap rhythms and ask children to repeat them.

- Memorize poems, nursery rhymes, songs, finger plays and Bible thoughts.

- "Guess Who?" is a commercial game that supports memory and reverse classification.

- Play board games. Children learn to remember rules.

Impulse Control

Impulse control can be defined as the capacity to resist the urge to act upon every thought or emotion. A friend of mine once had a particularly challenging student who struggled in the area of impulse control. She rearranged the student's desks often, trying to find the perfect arrangement that might help this child to stay focused and in control of himself. The following letter was written by another eight-year old to this challenging boy when she realized she would be sitting next to him for a few days:

Dear Nathan,
I am happy to share this space with you; however, there are a few things I need from you.

Please respect yourself.
Please keep your stuff off the floor and not in my space.
Please don't distract me with your talking.
If you agree to do these things, please sign here

_____.

    Your friend,
    Callie

You can see in these few words the contrast between a child with a high degree of impulse control and one who is struggling. Lack of impulse control impacts children socially as well as emotionally. During group times, Nathan blurts out answers to every question, ignoring the teacher's instructions to raise his hand and take turns. He pokes other children with his pencil, gets out of his chair to wander the room when he is supposed to be working on a group project and butts in front of other children to take a turn on the swing.

After a particular trying day he was asked to go sit in a rocking chair with the hope that it would help him to calm down and collect himself. When the teacher wasn't looking, he pulled out a pair of scissors, cut several chunks out of his hair then proceeded to sprinkle the hairs on one of his classmates. Needless to say, his actions caused a minor riot and the exasperated teacher sent him to the office for a visit with the principal. While waiting in the office, the secretary stepped out for a moment and the child called 911 to report a robbery. As you can imagine, this didn't go over well with the principal nor the police department. Nathan acts upon every thought or emotion that he feels.

When it comes to teaching children how to control their impulses, modeling is the key. Children aren't always very good at listening but they are experts at imitation. When my daughter was in middle school she said to me one day, "I hate it when you are stressed because it makes me feel stressed too." Those were sobering words to hear. Emotions are contagious and children "download" the emotional states of their parents. Children need to see mom and dad control their own emotions and manage their impulses appropriately. If you are prone to angry outbursts, so will your child. If you are an impulsive shopper, chances are your child will also become one. Children are keen observers and imitators of adult behavior.

One of the first steps to impulse control is helping children learn to identify and name their emotions. Throughout the day, identify and name your own feelings. "I'm really happy because Aunt Carol is coming for a visit." "I am really frustrated because I have a flat tire and I have a doctor's appointment in an hour."

Hang the language on your child's emotions. When Johnny lets out a yelp when trying to get his block tower to stay up say, "Wow…you're really frustrated. Need some help?" When we can identify a feeling we are more likely to be able to control it. If it is just some vague sense of "yuckiness" it is more difficult to know what to do with it.

A key understanding that children need to be taught is that they aren't to blame for what they feel but they are responsible for what they do with that feeling. All feelings are valid but not all actions are appropriate. We have learned from brain research that we have little control over what we feel but we do have control over what we do with the feeling.

Help your child learn appropriate ways to manage strong emotion. Adults often forget this step. We tell children to stop yelling, stop crying or stop jumping on the couch when they are excited but we typically neglect to tell them what they **can** do. For example, "It's not okay to jump on the couch when you are excited, but it's okay to jump on the floor, clap your hands or dance." "When you are frustrated, throwing a temper tantrum isn't going to solve the problem. You can take some deep breaths to help yourself calm down and then ask for help." "When you are angry it's not okay to throw things against the wall. You can use the sit 'n spin for five minutes or bounce on the trampoline to help yourself calm down." Developing this kind of self-control takes time and patience and continual practice. When your child slips up and demonstrates inappropriate impulse control, don't punish. Give them a do-over. "It's not okay to scream when you are frustrated. Let's try that again." You might have to remind your child many times what appropriate behavior looks like. Rational thinking shuts down when we experience strong emotion.

We live in a world of instant gratification. We zap our meals in microwaves, eat fast food and complain when our internet doesn't pop up within five seconds. We don't do "waiting" very well. Neither do our children.

I was in the emergency room with my husband one afternoon. I'd rather lay on a bed of nails than sit in an emergency room. I thought emergencies called for speed but this is apparently not so. I think emergency rooms across America need to be renamed, "Waiting Area" or "Endurance Room."

On this particular afternoon a Mom and a Dad came in with their two children—a boy and a girl who were probably eight and ten respectively. Despite the fact that we were the only ones in the area the wait was looooooong—two hours long. I amused myself by pretending to read a magazine but I was actually paying more attention to the interactions of this family.

By the way...yes, if you see me in public I am probably watching you. I am fascinated by human behavior and the world is my laboratory. The boy twisted and turned in his chair, backwards, forwards, sideways and upside down. Once he tired of the chair gymnastics he began to flick his sister whenever she looked away from him. This resulted in a tense two minutes of a stare down with the girl finally shrieking, "He's lookin' at me!" Dad puffs out his chest and says, "Boy, I'm gonna take you to the truck," with an accent that is unmistakably Okie. The boy spins around in his chair and sits quietly for about five seconds and then proceeds to make faces at his sister. You get the picture.

This went on for two hours with the Dad periodically awakening from his trance and threatening to take the kid to the truck. I wanted to scream, "play a game with him… invent a word game, play I Spy…tic tac toe…anything other than utter idle threats and sit there like a bump on a pickle."

There are many times throughout the school day when children will be expected to wait for short periods of time and they need to be taught how. It doesn't just happen. Take advantage of the everyday moments of life and help your child develop some strategies for waiting:

- When you are standing in line at the grocery store, play "I Spy," read the titles of magazines on the racks or the candy wrappers on the shelf; count the items in your basket as you put them on the counter.

- While riding in the car listen and sing to children's music, play word games, read signs and billboards and tell stories.

- Make a "writing to go box" to take with you in the car. Fill it with an assortment of paper, markers, stickers, a hole punch and other interesting writing materials. Take it with you to doctor appointments.

- Have a small backpack of books on hand, ready to take with you on trips in the car and to places your children may have to wait

- Have a backpack of small interactive toys such as a small etch-a-sketch, magic slate, flannel board and flannel shapes or string games for children to play.

Chapter Eight

Curiosity

When my daughter was two years old she had a "big wheel" trike she loved riding. It had a little compartment behind the seat that often contained her "treasures." One day as I stood outside with other moms, watching our kids ride their bikes up and down the street, I noticed her stopping every now and then, picking something up and putting it in the compartment. Engrossed in her own little world I quietly walked closer to see what she was gathering. Much to my surprise, she was picking up cicadas. When I looked into the trunk of her big wheel she probably had a hundred bugs stored inside in.

Children, boys and girls alike, are fascinated by creepy crawly things. Snails, grasshoppers, rollie pollies, caterpillars, ladybugs and ants, spark children's curiosity and wonder about the world. Many experts believe that curiosity is the primary motivating factor in learning. I would agree. I've met a few children along the way who have had curiosity squeezed right of them. The absence of joy, the dull vacant look in their eyes robs them of the spontaneity of youth. Babies are born with enormous curiosity and we squeeze it out of them by making inappropriate demands, throwing technology at them or insisting on perfection.

The child's drive to master the world is fueled by an innate sense of curiosity about the world and how it works.

The parent of any preschooler has been asked, "Why?" more times than they can count. It is an indication that they are trying to make sense of things. Take a child's "Why?" question seriously. The inquisitiveness of children often taxes the knowledge of even the most knowledgeable adult. Don't be afraid of admitting that you don't know the answer to their question. We now have the world at our fingertips and with the click of a mouse we can find information on just about anything. In finding answers together, parents model for children what it means to be a learner. They see mom and dad taking an interest in the world and learning new things. This sends a powerful message to any child.

Take time to explore the natural world with your child. Children have a natural affinity to the outdoor environment. I think this bent toward nature harkens back to our beginnings. We were created to live in a garden. The scriptures tell us that the natural world proclaims the glory of God and points us to Him. I believe the attraction children have for the natural world is an echo of our design, and the memory of our first home.

In days gone by, children could safely explore their neighborhoods and towns without constant adult supervision. Not so today. For most children, parents are going to have to make an intentional choice to introduce their children to the natural world. People with the financial ability to do so, take their children on vacations to different parts of the country and world. But you don't have to have lots of money to introduce the wonder of nature to your kids.

- Take a walk around your neighborhood and look for wildlife, birds and insects.

- Make bird feeders and learn about the birds in your area. Learn to identify them by sight and sound.

- Plant a garden. If space is limited, plant flowers or

vegetables in a flower pot. Or, simply break open a bag of peat moss and grow plants right in the bag.

- Cut out the eyes of a potato and plant it in the yard or in a pot.

- Put toothpicks around the mid-section of a sweet potato and submerge the bottom half in water. Watch the plant grow.

- Collect lightening bugs for children to examine. Let them go after they have had a chance to observe them up close.

- Allow your child to have a family pet. Learn about the pet's needs and habits so your child can adequately take care of it.

- Visit the zoo or a pet store.

- Gather leaves, twigs, acorns and other natural object around your neighborhood. Make a collage of natural objects. Paste can be made by simply mixing together flour and water.

- After a rain, go outside and look for worms on the pavement.

Chapter 9

Laying a Foundation for Math

The general public is well aware of the importance of reading to children. Schools and foundations have done a great job of educating the public on the benefits of storybook reading. As with most things, our society has a tendency to tip the scale in one direction to the exclusion of the other. This is true of math. The vast majority of preschool and kindergarten programs in America offer some kind of formal literacy instruction but only about 20% of programs offer any kind of intentional math experiences. Recent research indicates that high literacy scores in kindergarten predict high literacy scores throughout formal schooling. But high math scores in kindergarten predict high math AND literacy scores for the future. There are many ways that parents can teach math skills in ordinary, "day to day experiences"

- Use words of directionality and position. When children are playing on a playground parents use words of directionality: climb UP the slide, run AROUND the tree; put the ball IN FRONT of you, etc. Words that indicate a position or direction are part of what we call math vocabulary. Look for ways to include these words in ordinary conversation.

- Play board games. Candy Land, Chutes and Ladder, Hi-Ho Cherry-O, Guess Who?, Hungry, Hungry Hippo and

Go Fish are a just a few of the games on the market for young children. These games expose children to counting, number lines, number recognition and classification.

- Take advantage of ordinary moments to give your child opportunities to count. Ask them to count how many napkins are needed for dinner; how many cookies are needed for snack; or how many towels are needed for a trip to the pool.

- Sorting items into categories is another important skill. Ask your child to sort the canned goods into categories: fruit, vegetables, soups, canned meats. Sort the fruits and vegetables in the refrigerator drawers; sort socks; sort clothes into light and dark, wearing clothes and sheets and towels. Sort shoes, scarves, hats or toys.

- Point out patterns that they encounter in daily life: rugs, clothing, buildings, fabric, ceilings and nature. Go on a pattern walk in your neighborhood and look for patterns in houses, fences, signs, streets and nature. Look at the patterns in stained glass windows found in some churches.

- Point out shapes found in ordinary items such as books, plates, balls, shoe boxes or a piece of pizza.

- Help your child make simple foods and snacks that involve following a recipe and measuring.

- Give your child a tape measure that clips onto their waistband or belt. They will measure everything in sight. They obviously won't measure accurately, but they will "approximate" measuring much like they sit in the driver's seat and approximate driving a car.

- Create musical patterns with different sounds such as clap, snap, snap, stomp. Have your child repeat them.

Dr. Barbara Sorrels

- Learn simple songs with numbers such as *The Ants Go Marching One by One or There Were Ten in a Bed.*

- Make your own counting books by cutting out pictures from magazine or drawing.

- Estimate how many hops it will take to get to the door; how many rolls will fit into the basket or how many Hershey kisses are in the candy jar.

You will notice that most of the activities I suggest doing with your child involve mostly free or inexpensive materials. The one exception I'm going to make is blocks. I'm talking about the wooden blocks that we call "unit" blocks. They are cut proportionately so that two squares equals one rectangle; two small rectangles equals one large rectangle; two triangles equals one square, etc. Building with unit blocks is one of the best mathematical experiences you could provide. Research indicates that the capacity to build complex block structures at age four predicts high math scores through high school. If your budget allows, this is well worth the investment.

Chapter 10

Literacy

Some of my favorite memories with my children involve books. When my girls were very young I used to read a book to them called, *"Five Minutes Peace."* It is the story of a family of elephants. Mrs. Large, the mom, has had a hectic day and wants just five minutes of peace so she gets in the bathtub and settles back for a moment of relaxation. She is soon joined by all three of her children for various reasons and they all end up in the bathtub with her.

One night, after a particularly trying day, my husband, who happens to be a quadriplegic, was in bed as were the children. I retreated to the patio out back for a few moments of quiet. Thinking that the girls were asleep, I was startled to hear the pitter patter of little feet coming toward me. My three year old appeared, carrying her favorite stuffed doll. I sighed...so much for a moment of alone time. She perched next to me on the porch swing and innocently asked, "Are you trying to get five minutes peace?" I nodded and couldn't help but smile at the reference to the book. Looking very pleased with herself she replied, "Well, I've come to get five minutes peace with you!"

Favorite stories from childhood become woven into the fabric of our lives and become part of ordinary conversation with our children. Words from Robert Munch's book, *I'll Love You Forever,* was often heard around our house and often interjected a bit of light heartedness into tense situations. On the eve of my daughter's sixteenth birthday she had a serious lapse in judgment that resulted in a two month long delay in taking her driving test. She shed a great deal of tears over her transgression as she realized the seriousness of her error and our disappointment. As she headed to bed that night she paused on the stairs, turned to me and quietly asked, "Mom, do you still love me?" I quoted the beloved words of Robert Munch, "I'll love you forever, I'll like you for always. As long as I'm living my baby you'll be." She smiled and sniffled her tears away and said, "Awww...gee, thanks, Mom."

Books acquaint children with concepts, people and worlds that they would never encounter in ordinary life. They teach values and allow children to encounter role models that can inspire for a lifetime. And they expose children to important literacy skills that prepare the way for success in reading. It takes about two thousand interactions with print before children learn that lines and squiggles on a page carry meaning. Until children are able to grasp this notion, the print they see on a page is nothing more than black marks on a sheet of paper. There are many ways throughout the day to engage children in these important interactions:

- Invite your child to help make grocery lists or other lists for shopping and remembering. They can draw pictures of needed items and you can write the words.

- Point out "environmental" print. What is the first sign or symbol most American children recognize? For most children it is McDonalds! The implications of this are debatable but the up side is that recognition of the golden arches is often a child's first encounter with a printed symbol that carries meaning. This is the foundation of literacy. There are many ways to engage children with environmental print and contribute to the quantity of meaningful interactions required. Point out street signs, billboards, signs and symbols on businesses and food packaging. Collect napkins from favorite restaurants. As you walk the aisle at the grocery store, ask your toddler or preschooler to look for the Cheerios, or their favorite brand of soup or juice.

- Cut the front off food packaging and make puzzles.

- Allow your child to cut pictures of favorite things out of magazines and glue them into a scrapbook. The book can be made by simply folding and stapling blank sheets of paper together. If the items aren't already labeled, write the name of each object under the picture.

- As you read to your toddler, sweep your finger under the line of print so that they begin to understand that you are reading the black print on the page and not the pictures. Young children often think you are reading the pictures instead of the words. They also learn that print moves from top to bottom and left to write.

- Write your child's name on their belongings and on any scribblings or drawings they may do. Point out the letters of their name.

- Retell and act out your child's favorite stories.

- Tell stories from your own childhood. Children love to hear stories about Mom and Dad growing up.

Chapter Eleven

Social Skills

The classroom is a relational laboratory and requires the capacity to navigate relationships between both peers and adults. Knowing how to be a friend and make a friend is an important readiness skill. Children need to know how to share, take turns, negotiate, and give compliments and apologies. Research indicates that children who have meaningful friendships do better academically in school, enjoy school more and are more likely to graduate than those who are lacking social skills.

The capacity to engage in social relationships begins in infancy. Mom is typically the baby's first playmate and play during infancy is just as important as milk. Around four months of age the Gerber Baby shows up and begins to initiate playful interactions. Ordinary childhood games such as "peek-a-boo" or "pat-a-cake" teach the child about the give and take of relationships. Rolling a beach ball back and forth is the first step to turn taking. As babies become mobile their play becomes increasingly active and they often invite their caregivers to join in. They will enjoy playing "chase" and "hide-and-go-seek" and other high-energy games. These are the first steps in the journey toward socialization.

I was working in an infant center during grad school and a Mom walked in just as her eight-month-old grabbed a rattle from the baby who was lying on a blanket next to her. Mom became very upset, yelled at the baby and exclaimed, "I can't believe I have a child that doesn't know how to share." I pulled her aside and explained to her that children don't typically learn how to take turns until they are around three-years-old and only after lots of practice. Children will need consistent guidance when it comes to learning how to share and take turns. These are capacities that evolve over time and not over a day or a week. Sometimes we confuse children by inappropriately using the words "share" and "take turns" interchangeably. I can share a cookie but I can't share a toy. I can share the play dough but I can't share a bike. Parents need to make sure children know what to say when they want a turn or want someone to share with them. Simply say, "This is how we do it. May I please have a turn with the bike?"

One day, as I was visiting a shelter for foster children, two little boys got in a fight over a toy phone. Carl grabbed it out of Daniel's hand and demanded, "Give me that." This instigated a knock-down-drag out between the two boys who were both squalling. I was sitting on the floor nearby and sat them down, one boy on each knee. "That's not how we do things," I said. "Carl, this is what you say when you want a toy: 'Daniel, may I please have a turn with the phone.' Say that to Daniel." As he dried his tears he complied and asked for a turn. Daniel emphatically said, "No." A legitimate answer.

"Carl, this is what you say next: 'Daniel, when you are finished with the phone will you let me know so I can have a turn?'" Children need to know that asking politely for a toy doesn't guarantee or obligate the other child to release it. Teach them to respond by saying, "Will you let me know when you are finished so I can have a turn?"

By the time a child enters formal schooling, he needs to know how to enter into group play. The primary reason that children are excluded from play is that they don't know how to become part of an existing theme and they attempt to hijack the play and redirect it to their own goals. For example, a group of four year olds were playing "pizza shop." Marc suddenly barged into the middle of the shop and loudly proclaimed, "I'm batman!" as he knocked the "pizzas" off the table and tripped over the sign. The play came to a halt with angry protests. Then the self-appointed "queen bee" said, "You can't play with us. Go away." Marc experienced the angry rejection of his peers one more time.

Children like Marc need adults to become their play partner and teach them how to play. "What kind of pizza do you like, Marc? Pepperoni? Cheese? Sausage? Let's go order one. This is what you say....." Step by step, children who struggle need to be coached through a play scene much like a child is coached to play team sports.

The first five years of life is the "prime time" for learning social skills. If a child has not learned how to be a friend and make friends by the time he enters school, the odds are that he will continue to struggle socially throughout his school career. Children who lack this capacity are typically seen as behavioral "problems" and are usually punished or sent to time out for their transgressions.

Chapter Twelve

The Right Start

In many preschools, childcare centers and Head Start programs across the country there is a single-minded focus on teaching children letters, numbers, colors, sounds and shapes. If the children in their care can do these things then it is assumed that the teachers have done their job and the children are "ready" for school. I hope you realize by now that this is not the case. Readiness is much bigger than skills. With that said, however, it does not mean that skills are unimportant. I liken it to building a house. Skills are much like the frame of a house. The framework makes it possible to actually build the house. Skills provide the basic structure upon which more complex understandings of the world are built.

When it comes to learning skills, how we teach is just as important as what we teach. Skills need to be taught in terms of something meaningful to the child. For example, our understanding of how children learn the alphabet has changed over the years. We now know that the first letters most children learn to identify are the letters in their name. Why? Because their name is meaningful to them and it gives them a "context" in which to make sense of these symbols that we call letters. And typically, when children are in print rich environments, the next letters they learn are those in the words, "Mom" and "Dad" or the names of their friends or siblings. These are words that carry meaning to them. If I try to teach the alphabet to a child by drilling them with flash cards, it will take many, many repetitions for the information to stick because there is no meaningful context to attach the information.

Or, take colors for instance. There are computer games that are basically electronic worksheets. Pictures flash on the screen and a robotic voice says, "click on the red object." This is an example of an isolated drill. But when I say, "I like the pretty pink bow in your hair." Or, "You used a lot of purple in your picture today," I am teaching color in the context of something that is important to the child and the brain has a mental hook upon which to hang the knowledge.

When we teach something in a meaningful context it takes four or five repetitions. When we teach something out of context, some experts believe it can take as many as four-hundred repetitions. So what skills are important for children to know? What are appropriate expectations for children?

- Animal sounds. Most children can recognize animal sounds between 18 months and two years.

- Sounds in the environment. Most children can identify sounds in the environment around two years of age.

- Colors. Most children in a language rich environment can identify colors by two or three years.

- Shapes. Most children can identify basic shapes--circle, square, rectangle and triangle by age three.

- Most children can sort a set of simple objects by age three.

- Rhyming words. Most children can identify rhyme by age four.

- Name. Most children can recognize their name by age four and most will be able to write it.

- Most children can follow a two-step direction by age four.

- Number sense. Most children can form sets of objects through number five by four years of age.

Summary

When it comes to school readiness we need to think in terms of giving children a right start instead of a head start. Learning is a function of nurture. Well-nurtured children are the result of loving and attentive parents. Dr. Karyn Purvis says, "The cost of the human brain is three years of tender nurture."

If we invest in the well-being of our children and make their growth and development our priority in the early years, we will not have to spend the rest of their lives trying fix and undo the effects of our inattention and neglect. Love well.

There is no fear in love;
but perfect love casts out fear.

I John 4:18

For more helpful insights about nurturing the hearts of children, please see our web site, and subscribe to our free newsletter.

www.DrBarbaraSorrels.com

Contact us to discuss having Dr. Barbara speak at your conference, church, or event.

References

GEORGES, A., BROOKS-GUNN, J., & MALONE, L. (2011). Links between young children's behavior and achievement: The role of social class and classroom composition. American Behavioral Scientist. Retrieved from http://abs.sagepub.com/content/56/7/961.full.pdf+html

LIEBERMAN, A. (1993). The emotional life of the toddler. New York: The Free Press.

NEUFELD, G., & MATÉ, G. (2006). Hold on to your kids: Why parents need to matter more than peers. New York: Ballantine Books.

PERRY, B. (2001). Curiosity: The fuel of development. Retrieved from http://teacher.scholastic.com/professional/bruceperry/curiosity.htm

RILEY, D., SAN JUAN, R., KLINKNER, J., & RAMMINGER, A. (2008). Social and emotional development: Connecting science and practice in early childhood settings. St. Paul, MN: Redleaf Press.

WALKER, A., & MACPHEE, D. (2011). How home gets to school: Parental control strategies predict children's school readiness. Early Childhood Research Quarterly, 26, 355–364.

Made in the USA
Charleston, SC
11 March 2017